ENDURING FREEDOM

A Little Book of Mechanical Brides

LAURA MULLEN

OTIS BOOKS | SEISMICITY EDITIONS

The Graduate Writing program
Otis College of Art and Design
LOS ANGELES ● 2012

Book design and typesetting: Rebecca Chamlee

ISBN-13: 978-0-9845289-8-1

ISBN-10: 0-9845289-8-9

OTIS BOOKS | SEISMICITY EDITIONS
The Graduate Writing program
Otis College of Art and Design
9045 Lincoln Boulevard
Los Angeles, CA 90045

http://www.otis.edu/
http://gw.otis.edu/
https://blogs.otis.edu/seismicity/

"Well, on to the slaughter."

(GOODRICH AND HACKETT, <u>FATHER OF THE BRIDE</u>, 1950)

To those in the Theater of Operations

Seating Chart

With

the kiss of white on white
pages the book shuts a bride-
to-be dreams her dress a deep
pile of ashes the wind lifts
unfurling the long pale flag of
shreds to lace and then
this red incoherence the few
stuttered vanishing words
of the service dust to dust
the shadow of meanings cast
over these open snowfields
after the weeping faithless
reader through whose burning
eyes what lies ahead passes

Shower
(A WAR CEREMONY: SPRING 2003)

Stay with us: fictitious negotiations for access to prisoners on television ongoing. Where do you get your numbers? "I'm wearing a tuxedo." "They're surrendering gleefully." A region considered unsafe accepting art is important. "Don't do anything you'd look back on and be disturbed by." Continue to burn continuing uncertainty: "a self-declared buffer zone." Syria is next the awards are next: "Violence inevitably leads to more violence." 45 seconds before the orchestra to remind them to check on their well-being. Showed a white flag described as "disgusting." Someone rifling the pockets of the dead smiled at the camera – the element of surprise the envelope please.

Accepting again they won't have any effect. "I've been hit, I've been shot." How is the conflict perceived? It's a powerful image in diamonds amazing embedded in a conference warning us welcome many people staying away. "Once war begins fiction takes over." Be prepared for more news like this: how do we block communication? We have people out there who would apparently like to do harm to us we have family. Waterless tomb center of resistance theme music special coverage. This critical time. Experts and eye-witnesses extending under the city out into the desert. "What is terrorism but the arm of despair?" The coverage is another reason to remove the regime.

"All free people puppets isolated fear the enemy beaten and buried." Singers entertain guests on the banks of the Nile. "What are you wearing?" / "Who are we killing?" The danger that they will repeat what they are told to say. The next award presented by a digitally created character wearing a tuxedo I picked up in a charity shop to serve as a guarantee of peace and stability. Stay with us we're afraid to appear frivolous in this economy. Still to come: how the war is affecting the ceremony. What is art for? The exile community waiting anxiously. There's a split personality inside everyone the big problem is how to strike the right tone. "Hey, don't feel sorry for *them* – remember they were shooting at *us*!" *And the winner is...*

"The invitation."

She should be seen speaking from under a dress halted in being settled on her (as we say) frame, meaning she can't be seen speaking. A promise muted her and their to mumble seems to emerge only at moments from layers of material. Her arms straight up in the air as if in waving her hands above this over-whelming froth of white as if (as if she were drowning in foaming soap bubbles) she'd signal. But what words might be heard in this blank would be blurred and resemble a bird call. Pure music mere sound all materiality and of course beautiful beautiful beautiful... And something (this glittering fabric twitched won't lift or descend but stays like this, a sort of waterfall as if she's caught inside a waterfall as if she were the speaking spirit of a waterfall, drowned in sound, but generating a current so powerful...) something something word obscured in the shining churn of substances not biodegradable...so she should be seen (meaning she can't be seen) engaged, as we say, in something of a struggle...

Bride Space

Hollow and larger than life-size, the BS invites entrance ("he entered her") though of course there are rumors that the voluminous folds of that colorless dress bedecked with bleached flowers conceal quagmires, and we've all heard that not everyone who goes in comes out again. You told me that story, I think: you told me you'd heard it from someone who'd heard it from someone who knew someone who…went there, yes? But it's true that the silence in the gown – despite busloads of tourists – remains "profound." There are always lonely corners where you can vow (with a distant whispered echo) to love forever in sickness and so forth, your blush (if suspected) well hidden in the gloom. It's a little dank: you'll want to wrap yourself well in these proffered synthetics, taking advantage of the flowing white ponchos – available for a nominal fee – of Banlon and Bridalace. All visitors to the BS are given flashlights disguised as bouquets: silhouettes of blown roses and broken baby's breath cross and blur on the high blank walls; there are also those huge glowing Lucite "solitaire" rings for purchase, if you're uneasy about setting off alone in the increasing dimness. Thawing slices of vanilla cake slathered in butter-cream (each in a monogrammed doggie bag) are stacked on a table by the door: take one in case you do get lost. No one who's been once would need to return, would they? I think you asked me that but maybe you were quoting somebody who'd asked somebody else. Rumors of a discovery whose urgent importance is measured by the frequency with which it can be repeated (oh happy happy etc.) mostly prove to be false, or it seems as if the discoverer – sooner or later – turns out not to be who we all thought it was but someone else: someone who, just recently, seems to have vanished…along with the funding for research and development.

Headstone

"He buried himself within her."

Pride Bride

She is a truth universally acknowledged and the only handsome girl in the room (with something more of quickness than her sisters). The business of her life is to be married and to that business we proceed? "'I can guess the subject of your reverie.'" As if the credit for making it rain were all her own! Will you give me leave to defer your raptures? She is perfectly serious in her refusal, she is not romantic, she never was. "'Well...have it as you choose. *He* shall be mercenary and *she* shall be foolish.'" Who can afford to marry without some attention to money? It was gratifying to have inspired unconsciously so strong an attraction. Had her opinion been all drawn from her own family, she could not have formed a very pleasing picture of conjugal felicity or domestic comfort, but it is many months since I have considered her one of the handsomest women of my acquaintance. Her affections had been continually fluctuating, but never without an object. The bride and her mother could neither of them talk fast enough. I think there cannot be too little said on the subject. We all love to instruct though we can teach only what must have taken place with that gentleman's concurrence. The PB is certainly the most fortunate creature that ever existed, in spite of that pollution which its woods had received.

Bride of the Detail

The fold in the napkin we're working on now is called a "love knot." If you don't start it correctly the unfinished edge will face up – much less pleasant to approach don't you think. I thought so. Roses, you know, gasp for air when cut: the blades should close under water, actually. She squints then she frowns, the BD, trying to see not only what we will see but what we might see. Any petals that fall off the blossoms we're wiring today should be saved and refrigerated for tossing but only if they are PERfect. Hand-stitched and beaded by little women far away (living in factory dormitories, dreaming of better lives for the children they rarely see), the gown should almost look as if you made it yourself; it should be kept in the refrigerator until the last possible moment; it's a little bit time-consuming but completely worth it. Each guest can be given a grain of rice engraved with the date and your new initials. A full moon adds to the ambiance, and little votives stuck in the eye sockets make this arrangement just magical. It should look as if you can command the kind of dedicated labor that built the pyramids, only there shouldn't be even a whiff of sweat about it, if you know what I mean. Just a faint scent of glue-gun over the stench of trust fund – that's what we're going for here: just a few simple, elegant ideas. She puts on reading glasses she quickly replaces with bifocals she discards in favor of a jeweler's loup and then a magnifying lamp. The crease in the leaf we're working on now ensures there isn't any trace of the Styrofoam peeking through – much nicer, don't you think. In the Styrofoam's stiff blank glitter you can foresee the wandering and erratic care of the distracted wife and the dangerously neglectful mother. (You'll want help with some of this.) Between the exquisite blue feathers we're pinning jade flowers studded with tanzanite, and then we're adding a variety of little trophies. This is the kind of attention to detail that can really set the tone for your invasion, I mean conflict, I mean occupation. It should look as if it came from your own garden, there shouldn't be anything fussy about it. We can't see what she's seeing but we can see the increasing effort to look – how it involves not just her eyes, but (first her jaw and neck, then her shoulders thrust forward) her whole body. It should look as if you pillaged the wealth of the east, but there shouldn't be a touch of anything slavish about it, if you know what I mean. The hoods should be simple, a soft black cloth snipped on the bias, or forest green plastic, or, for a change, use women's panties paired with contrasting cables: what's important is that it should look as if you could've done it all yourself. Most importantly, you don't want the leaves touching the water, they soften and rot which is not a nice smell at all. If you do it right it gives you this beautiful sense of life; it's modern and classic. After that it's a breeze. Setting aside the binoculars to watch us assemble surveillance equipment, the BD winds up, as the song puts it, peeking through a keyhole down upon her knees. The contemporary bride knows all of this: she comes into the shop with a portfolio of dreams.

Bride of Some Operation Names (A-L)

Abilene, Able Warrior, Airborne Dragon, All American Tiger, Alljah, Antica Babilonia, Arctic Sunrise, Ardennes, Arrowhead Blizzard, Arrowhead Ripper, Arrowhead Strike III, 9 and 10, Badlands, Backbreaker, Bastille, Baton Rouge, Bayonet Lightning, Beastmaster, Black Eagle, Black Shark, Black Typhoon, Block Party and Block Party II, Bold Action, Bone Breaker, Boothill, Bowie, Bruins, Bulldog, Bulldog Mammoth, Cajun Mousetrap II and III, Catalyst, Centaur Fast Gas, Centaur Rodeo, Centaur Showdown, Centaur Strike II and III, Chamberlain, Checkmate, China Shop, Chokehold, Church, Clear Area, Clear Decision, Clean Sweep, Cobra Strike, Cobra Sweep, Cobweb, Combined Justice, Commando Eagle, Constant Solidarity, Constitution Hammer, Dagger, Danger Fortitude, Dawn, Dealer, Desert Farewell, Desert Scorpion, Desert Snowplow, Desert Thrust, Destroyer Strike, Devil Clinch, Devil Siphon, Dirty Harry, Dragon Fire and Dragon Fire East, Dragon Hammer, Dragon Victory, Dragons Breath, Duke Fortitude, Duke Fury, Duliyah Sunrise, Eagle Claw XI, Eagle Curtain, Eagle Ares, Eagle Dive I, Eagle Liberty 3, Eagles, Eagle Shiloh III, Eagle Sweep, Eagle Venture IV, Enduring Freedom, Falconer, Falcon Freedom, Falcon Fury, Falcon Sweep, Final Strike, Gator Inn, Gimlet Crusader, Gimlet Silent Sniper, Gladiator, Glad Tidings of Benevolence II, Glory Light, Great Lakes, Grizzly Forced Entry, Guardian Tiger IV, Guardian Torch, Haifa Street, Hickory View, Hermes, Hurricane & Hurricane II, Industrial Revolution, Industrial Sweep, Iraqi Freedom, Iron Arrow II, Iron Blitz, Iron Bullet, Iron Fist II, Iron Force, Iron Fury and Iron Fury II, Iron Grip, Iron Hammer, Iron Harvest, Iron Justice, Iron Reaper, Iron Roundup II, Iron Saber, Iron Triangle, Ithaca, Ivy Blizzard, Ivy Cyclone, Ivy Cyclone II, Ivy Lancer Fury, Ivy Needle, Iron Promise, Iron Resolve, Ivy Serpent, Jaws V, Justice League, Keystone Sweep, Lightning, Lightning Blitz, Lightning Hammer and Lightning Hammer II, Lion, Lion Hunt and Lion Hunt II. Lions, Lions Roar, Longhorn, Longstreet....

Bride of the Lists

Dum duhm de dum, here she comes... Look out (don't *miss...*) Our
Lady of the "To-Do" Lists! A collection of held breaths or proof
of their measured release, she must be admired, not "mussed."
Drawing (Ta-Da!) a line or two through everything accomplished:
~~Fall in love~~. The trick is to *seem* natural – not be it! *Did* that! Light
and shadow cast a dense net across a crumpled slip smoothed out
where spiky verticals emerge above and below the hard horizon
where all that done (to death) stuff looks now like (eroding)
marsh grasses, fragile little islands, stacked... Finished! And her
dress is embroidered (in silk and seed-pearls) with "precisely"
that motif – white on white: ~~Get engaged~~. *Check!* Isn't it just this
just-do-it-just-did-it agenda we're reading everywhere, spelled
out in the intricate floral arrangements and then again (in case
we missed it), in threads of licorice, on that huge glowing cake?
Oh, the numberless lists she made and made her way through!
Let's celebrate these signs of completed triumph, as if this were
the ending and not the start – oops.* ~~Marry~~. Get married! *Check!*
Next? ~~Follow the money~~! They rush away in a storm of falling
seeds – as if the roof of the car were tapped by countless impa-
tient pencils – ticking the rest of it off: down payment, mortgage,
interest, taxes, insurance...

---

* But I'm only an oafish archivist, setting out not just to find a print but
a foot in all that froth (where that wide white skirt makes one of us stand-
offish) and then a way to step on it: seeking the smudge of an erased mark,
looking for meanings gleaned from between the dark bars of their emphatic
strikings out...where that blank gown announces she will be touched because
she wasn't touched because she can't be touched and bling should be seen as
a sign that you have the cash you spent. "I don't get it!" Think twice.

Bride of the Dream of the Perfect Day

As if good weather meant, no, *were* wedded bliss: a series of stan-
dard phrases or married words, conjugal felicity for instance (*for
instance* for instance). Dark clouds can swirl like dirty tissue in an
overflowing toilet somewhere else for all she cares but here and
now Fine is the only forecast. There's a touch of blue the BDPD
always turns to, willing that bright bit to stretch from horizon to
horizon with maybe a few brushed-on wisps of cirrus for orna-
ment, purely decorative, maybe symbolic (fecundity, etc) – why
not? Into every rain a little life and so on, oops, I mean...but not
today, not on her day. So *away* with it, bad weather, along with
spills, miscalculations, iffy temper and anyone who can't – as
she puts it – get with the program: stuff it in a box labeled "Just
for today" or "Once." So much of what comprises the world as
we know it must be heavily, sometimes clumsily, packed up and
hefted off-stage "Just for today" – her *special* day. Luckily it's not
far to the wings where wars and storms are contained and every
kind of disaster (from the assassination of a country's leader to a
chipped nail) is stashed helter-skelter – we can stagger off there,
if we've had one too many, to toss our cookies on the lot. The
number of lives lost yesterday in that marketplace bombing and
the overthrow of an elected government? It's all stacked back here
somewhere with global warning oops *warming*, and the fear that
the divorced in-laws will make a scene or just refuse to be photo-
graphed. It's not that she doesn't understand that a stain from
the unbound stems of her garden bouquet on the hand-beaded
duchess satin of her dress is of less importance than not only
genocide but also the fender bender that may or may not have
given grandma a little whiplash on her way to the church: her
heart – as she puts it – *is in the right place*. But – just for today – all
the signs should drown in light, a dazzling compress meaning
everyone's blind to everything except her beauty and happiness.
Surely that isn't too much to ask? Not here and not now she
admonishes the lack of potable water in the refugee camps and

her nephew sneaking off to the cloakroom again complaining there's no way to get through this without.... No no *no*! Portents: droopy roses mean there were abuses of detainees, cracked stemware and stained tablecloths are pretty much a confession that the number of civilian deaths was much higher than we thought. This line of green spots down her white skirt is just another indication that, even if the pre-nup negotiations didn't kill all affection, the parties involved were left distrustful and lawyered up. And rain and wind, for a storm announces itself (that turning wad of white in the Gulf), will come in, natural symbols, to say this coalition is unstable, that it was based on a lie, always, the whole long engagement.

Bride of the Photograph 1839-1930

In sepia the pressure of holding still too long reveals itself in compressed lips and flat blank stares, body and cloth seem equally stiff and the subjects resemble the period furniture: glossy and intended to be impervious to hard use. No one knows how to be recorded yet, no one knows how to act: for their transformation into image they are as earnest as painted supplicants at heaven's gate. Perhaps that is the key: they pose as if to be painted, in the image of the images of people on walls or canvas. But the pictures of the whole party are taken from such a distance the banked, expressionless faces seem like specks in a sort of landscape: birds nesting on eroding cliffs, perhaps, as glimpsed from the deck of a ship. At first the clothes are simply clean or "nice": there is no rule about apparel, and even by the end of this period the bride's dress is not always white. Gradually profusions of flowers, slowly the emergence of the candid shots: the subjects at last turn away from the camera, more involved with the moment than the future (what future?), or just beginning to understand that they have been called upon to present themselves to an unknown audience who will see them not simply as loved ones or ancestors but as dramatic figures more or less successful at representing the emotions understood to be appropriate. It takes almost a century for the lovers to look at each other, but in its first appearance the gesture already seems cited, as if the echo of the photographer's encouragement is just now fading out. And then a flower girl, wearing feathered wings and leading a couple yoked by a wide pale satin ribbon, lifts a little bow and arrow and gives us a defiant, slightly exasperated look. A sense of theater has begun to seep into and dissolve this site: the subject will soon be art itself. Cupid's charges, eyes lowered, heads bowed, seem like sleepwalkers led toward a precipice. Finally (after the invention of "moving pictures") stiff smiles: the presentation of happiness; then the bride cheek to cheek – against the mirror – with herself, the medium reveling in self-consciousness. And the bouquet flung from the departing ship, blossoms rocking in the wake (flowers at first almost indistinguishable from foam), breaks up, sinks, becomes a story not about foam or flowers, but about the oil-slicked water lapping at the dock – evidence of our effort to remember: proof of everything we are going to forget.

Bride of the Venue

Nothing like this has ever happened before reads the (invisible!) banner above the processional, a warning that the BV must be protected at every instant of her "special day" from knowledge of other ceremonies in progress. The notes of one "our song" must not blur into any alternative, nor the scent from one banquet flavor another, and guests who pretend to confusion in order to wander from production to production, as if in a megaplex, should be stripped of all cash and presents and summarily ejected. Everything here is "original," "unique" and "special" – and if you can't tell shocking pink from magenta you can leave that Cuisinart or crock pot on the table (with the others) and get out, thank you. *Nothing like this has ever happened before* or since. Chosen for its suitability, the venue's disastrous flaw is precisely this suitability: the hallways echo with heartfelt vows and the place is positively infested with stately processions, rollicking well-wishers, brides-maids in frocks they can't wait to get out of, and sulky children in soiled fancy dress. And brides, of course, but *don't* mention that! On the pole inscribed "Tradition" the BV's brave flag, rented for the occasion, flutters and snaps: *Nothing before.* She lowers her borrowed veil as if going into battle and though she knows her skirmish is part of a larger (on-going) conflict any actual confron-tation with proof of that fact is dangerous. The bride must *not*, under any circumstances, see another bride. She can see herself in a mirror, in one thousand mirrors – why not? – and (if he swears he won't just seize the chance to dump her), let her "one and only" also confront that crowd of exquisite reflections: his awe-struck face and stuttered *M-m-my* should keep her courage up. What she must be protected from is a confrontation with the wisdom she's being infected with: what is truly singular is a perfect reenactment. Her white attire marks a willful and precarious blankness (since *Nothing happened*) at the intersection of irreconcilable truths: each wedding is completely unique insofar as it resembles all others – *like this.*

Be Creative Bride

With a whirr and a thunk she edges forward, already begin-
ning to spin and to seem – as eyes and arms start to replicate
and stack – more than a little spider-like. Urged to express her
real self, expensively, to celebrate, in the phrase, her unique style,
the BCB's head swells to contain all the "bright ideas" she's sure
she'll be able to improve on yet essentially duplicate. It has to be
different, she wants it to be different, but it can't be too different:
my wedding, she insists, looking everywhere but at the groom
she's got wrapped in the sticky grip of You don't trust me do you
or You don't care or Can't you see that I'm doing all this for us for
us for us. She writhes and spins, dealing out the myriad charts
and samples, hissing the mantra: *What do you think what do you
think what do you...* The knife-blade descends on the stem of the
green jade flower or a finger; in airless rooms women rush to
finish the fabulous gown she swears she'll be able to wear (if I just
if I just...). Did she mention she has to lose a few pounds because
she's going to be brought in on a bower of bois dentelle blossoms
lifted by whooping cranes? Doesn't that sound just...meanwhile
the mad search for the exclusive videographer's number, scrawled
in lipstick on a vanished color swatch. Fuchsia? Peach? What
about green – that bright virescent shade, what's its name, darling,
alluring and poisonous? *What do you really think* punctuates each
description of her "innovations," varied with *Oh it's going to be
such a complete disaster* and *God it's got to be perfect. Choose choose
choose* is the chorus turning her until her many eyes glitter like
a pave diamond bandage, her countless arms blur into a sort of
ruff, and her blooming head (gaping mouth, undulant scribble
of hair) grows wider and wilder. Would you marry it marry it
marry it asks the poet. How will we ever pay for... – but *what do
you think* – it's my wedding. Occasionally she'll even interrogate
her immobilized groom – desperate! To take the silence any way
she wants. Under those spreading white skirts, so we've heard, a
crowd of pedicurists kneel to attend to the multitude of feet meant

to dance her (still twirling) to florists and caterers and department stores and – dance lessons! Meanwhile the high-pitched whine of her drill-like rotations: she's insisting just now his tuxedo be made of millerbird feathers and oh, copper wire; she's commissioning an ice sculpture (think Vietnam memorial!) for her seating chart – but all that could change, she assures us, in an instant. *Don't you think that's just…? I do!* At this point her special vows consist of a list of the places she's registered; but that's just a start. It's my wedding she explains…and it has to be original – surely we see that? Absolutely we say, it will be, and so *you*, really, we feel we really must at this point *must* reassure her. Really? *Oh we think so no we really really really think we think we do so so we do* and then we start to whirl ourselves until the rush and blur seem absolutely normal – *don't we don't I don't you…*

Gown Sound (Translated Bride)

("IF I WERE SWING MY MONEY")

There rattling is no artifact to provide a comely introduction: her designs are rank and amount! They are girly and feminine! They are tralatitious and ease unbelievably firm and innovative! Each eveningwear is a lowercase impact of prowess with alter overlays amend detailing and fabrics unabashedly luxe! I love love fuck Monique and if I were swing my money I'd feature you do too! Although she kept the aforementioned humanities ambiance her Fall 2010 had a some mythologic surprised! Traditional bodices word updated with fresh newborn shapes! Personal fade for the period definitely the meet above with lopsided bodice matched with artist alter protection and ballgown silhouette! Total me! It's actually a lowercase reminiscent of this eveningwear I wore for my possess ceremony which is essentially ground I fuck it so rattling much! I am also a lowercase taste in fuck with the eveningwear above, ordinal row! It's a silhouette tralatitious patch ease existence unbelievably sex! Layers and layers of artifact are a rank imagine and attain the whole countenance unbelievably princess! Love it! As usual, Monique completely impact discover of tract making me wager a lowercase taste fearless to play I am a bride again and essay on every azygos! Coming up next Priscilla! And to wager more from Monique utter correct here!

Bride of the Ways

She is essentially constructed of two columns of advice, each headed with some variation on "Splurge" and "Save." Ardently urged to spend her pennies, the BW is also primly admonished to try her grip on each gleaming copper surface. She should stay within her budget, but her budget should be ceaselessly revised. There's always someplace – someplace else – that a touch of strategic thriftiness might go unnoticed: such is the constant and constantly betrayed promise. Friends, family and colleagues are presented as eagle-eyed and unforgiving on one hand, and as myopic and understanding – if not unconscious – on the next. If it's true that each blossom in her bouquet can be replaced by something cheaper, and no one will ever notice... – it isn't clear how to reconcile that gospel with the unvarying caution: "Never stint on photographs!" But if that rented hall could be transformed into a magic forest...just by cutting dinner down to a couple of waiters fleeing through the greenery with snacks?! Her guest list shrinks to the few and to-be famished as she makes her "wise decisions," moving money from where, she's assured, a little less will be undetectable, to make (in another area) an "important statement." She can *cut corners*, she doesn't have to go *over the top*, though the sky high price of the astounding confection flown in from the atelier of a famous caterer is completely reasonable since the cake is "the big 'ta da' moment in the ceremony." Still, a frugal BW can always "find a good local bakery and call it a day" – if that's what she's like: while *Food is the heart of the event* it's understood that we can't all afford a heart. This all-too-ready acceptance of her inevitable failure rustles in the thinning foliage: the air is charged with the sympathetic clucking of those who assure her they're just sorry, really, really sorry she's stinting *herself.* The costly wedding she attempts to plan is so shadowed at every moment by the even more expensive affair it should be but isn't she shows the eyestrain of an innocent playing with a damaged stereoscope. At points the images seem almost, though jumping and trembling, to overlap – just to over-correct, so that saving begins to appear in every way less affordable than splurging – and then we find her passed out on the couch, lost under glossy pages dense with what now seem absurd, even cruel, suggestions (make your own cake, sew your own dress). And if, after all is said and done, it's just a matter of waving a little more plastic at the problem or dashing off one more signature on still another blank check...? Behind the pale and trembling bride is the resolute figure in red she resembles: she is given away by her debt.

Bride of the Flaw

In even the most perfect of days imperfections exist and the BF, going hungrily over the occasion, can give you the catalogue. Exact in her ability to recall every error or awkwardness, she has by heart each clumsy gesture and fashion mistake and she can cite, years later, each hastily spoken phrase that hurt her. Will you look, she repeats, pressing one hand down on the open album, at that?! And that and that... Leafing swiftly through friends and family, hastening to the ceremony itself: little jerk, she snarls, poking a ring-bearer all grown up by now – he told me I looked fat! She flings aside the heavy book, searches for the remote; I can't wait to get hold of *his* wife! In each glossy still her smile is tight: there's a not-so-subtle wariness on her happy face, as if she imagined us seeing then what she'll need, later, to point out. We're already too close: the BF (or BTF, that is, Bride of the Thousand Flaws, as she calls herself, with a short laugh) should be viewed from a distance, unless we're ready to be handed a list of what's wrong with *us*. Let me refill your glass. That's her with the wedding album held open in the video's flickering light, the TV on mute, one finger on a tiny crease of flesh in the back of the woman she was all those years ago, waiting for the yes. Look at *that*! We vowed to spend our lives with each other in our faulty bodies and defective spirits but we didn't know it would be like this. Is it our critique she attempts to head off? Can we see her as she sees herself: as just *saying it first*? Soliciting belated reassurances (she'll rush to dismiss)? She had to think of everything: from the safety pins in the "wedding emergency kit" to that ruffled swag of storm tacked on the edges of a hot sunset; every aspect to be foreseen by someone apparently at her ease in the eye of the whirling event, which it seems she maybe failed to experience. She turns up the volume and the voices of long gone giddy revelers fill the room, wishing her every kind of happiness. Look at them, she winces, gawd they're sooo drunk! Coming down the green aisle she was worrying about her hair and make up, recalling the location of blotting papers and band-aids, hoping the rain would hold off, her mostly interior monologue something like: *Grass-stains nothing I can do about Aunt Celeste always such a pain in the don't cry could still stand to lose a few*, I do, *my blemish...*

Gift Bride

"Easily assembled" from the assortment of objects presented to "the happy couple" "on this important occasion" ("the big day"), the GB is inevitably, in large part, a collection of clichés and duplicates. *Nobody's fool* is the phrase that occurs here to access her swift calculations as to what can be returned for cold hard cash. Crystal, silver, these words can be lifted and matched to her laugh. Registered and robotic, right on track: where the action of creating and cataloging desires opened the west. Bright and shiny "brand new" things make up the image of the future she located among the many items she was told to want, a golem's body all ill-fitting parts, few of which can in fact be afforded by her bewildered, docile, not rich (though anxious to seem so) guests. She moves stiffly against a certain resistance to tune the receiver to where matter catches the signal of the symbolic against the static of meaninglessness. Her distant look – glazed eyes, pale lips and distracted manner – a matter of uneasy frequencies and off-kilter clockworks. Something inside makes a soft click and drag as if checking off or crossing out products, a tiny sound drowned in the slither of her gown's cool gleaming fabric. Now and then a convulsive gulp: the GB is poison and poisoned, *thanks* her bitter drink. "What," she murmurs, beginning to wind down or maybe break, "shall we ever do with it." Attended closely by those who insist she deserves the best, whatever the cost, she practices an increasingly tentative perambulation through a narrowing and ever-more dangerous path. Pass – as in "it's come to such a...." The threat of collapse is ever-present in the rise – above drifts of loose cards and crumpled gift-wrap – of stacked and teetering things amid a tumble of broken Styrofoam shapes, crushed boxes, balled tissue, blister-pack and fluttering instruction booklets. Send it all back or shut your eyes, murmur another acknowledgement: *How thoughtful You shouldn't have Just what we wanted*. Wind her up and she hands you one more list or gestures again to the air repeating, "Look at this!" "Look at this." By the end the GB runs on guilt:

her hand moves ceaselessly (scratching an inkless pen across the desk's splintering surface) to inscribe an illegible gratitude she feels she might have felt or thinks someone in her position would or could have actually experienced, once.

Bride of the Diverse Rituals

"If the bride did not cry when she was married, her virtue was suspected: to prevent such censure, some arts were used to make her tears flow."

The Wedding Day in all Ages and Countries

Hefted over the threshold feigning unwillingness jangling keys dropped into the hand holding one end of the leash amid jests and obscene songs progress accompanied by tigers and guard dogs lifting the veil flinging a wreath of verbena gold threads bound by slender silk ribbons as shotguns are fired cakes tossed onto the quilt repeating felicitous sentences taken up by the company lighting our torch from hers as she rests on the skin of an ox a lamb the naked bodies of prisoners as water is poured over their faces as oil as handfuls of grain scattered doves flutter off and she's given away or sold and returns to her father's house for three days of chaste and austere living abstaining from salt and meditating on the bundle of sticks her bridesmaids voting again to increase the defense budget scratch the groom to keep him from carrying out his design as married female relatives share secret wisdom she's slapped with her husband's pants admonished to be fruitful and *Always ask for things after sex* then a red splatter as the chilled petals fall her responses bound to a certain number of cows coins candles a knife suspended from her skirt the forced accompaniment men dancing only with men and so forth secluded again a black or white veil knocked up or down knocked down and up

"Special moments during the ceremony."

She should be seen weeping, her face as the phrase goes *distorted by grief.* Wet slits of her almost shut eyes gaping hole of her howling mouth above the hard distended muscles of her throat. She should be seen like that – lost in what she expresses – from a distance and in silence. Face after face after face: her hair color changes, the tint of her skin the shape of her nose and the shade of those eyes we can barely glimpse through reddened, swollen lids...lashes matted and damp. What doesn't change is this: grief. Grief and despair and the space those emotions open between her ("broken-hearted") and us...if not actually laughing then certainly on our way to laughter as we pass. We pass seeing a number of different women or maybe all one woman "on a deep level" beloved but clearly (this is crucial to the experience) beyond our help. Clearly. She should be seen as transformed turned almost animal by sorrow – and hopelessness. I'm not sure our gaze goes farther than to register that the hands twisting in her lap are something less than perfectly clean as is now we look at it her lace skirt – and then we're on to something else. We're moving on we're moving forward we're getting on with things getting our lives back we're healing we've recovered almost completely we're better than ever only now we're a little wiser what doesn't as we say kill us and so forth. The weather the market a bird calling from a high leafless branch this or that celebrity getting married arrested divorced and wearing Totally the Wrong Outfit ha productivity levels and consumer confidence listen laughter this really (listen) really *excellent* joke...

Bride of the Dead

(DEAR... DAD)

Slightly muted by distance, this organ music (volume uncertain, long pauses between single notes or clumps of notes) has been going on for some time and still she does not move. Cobwebs link her long train to the moldering, dust-thick carpet but it is not their slight tension that makes her hesitate, nor the open question as to whether the wheezy, quavering music (stuck as it is in those opening bars) is a wedding or a funereal march: it's the arm linked through hers that holds her fast. She slides yet one more surreptitious glance to her elbow, crossed by another clad in the rusty moth-eaten black worsted of some long out of fashion "monkey suit." The withered hand emerging below the soiled cuff makes an ineffectual fist, blue-veined, age-spotted, a sort of mottled, friable rock wrapped in thin, crumpled, papery flesh. Her gaze flicks up once again to the front of the church before coming back to rest on her desiccated bouquet: at the other end of the aisle a bewildered almost stranger waits, a tumble of graying hair obscuring all but his wide and increasingly alarmed gaze. Who sees this? The brighter guests departed years ago and the officiant actually keeled over at some point and slid down to the floor, his or her face (who even recalls now?) obscured by a heavy book. Dum-dum-dum-dum goes the faltering but inexorable music. The BD flashes another quick glance of yearning at her groom—you know I would move if I could, her eyes say, darling, you know that...surely you see that it's...he won't let.... She's long past the stage of the girlish giggle and the flashing glance that said eloquently "Can you believe this!" or "What a fix!" And perhaps it's the fear that she'd bring, if she took a step forward, that arm alone, while the rest of whatever it was that had brought her to this point crumbled into a heap of ash—maybe that's what keeps her? She lifts her chin now and then as if ready to proceed but never turns to face what's left of the face of her escort. Sooner or later her groom must shut his eyes and turn on his heel, flipping the ring his vanished best man handed over into the dry font on his way out...the slammed door will probably turn Daddy into a wisp of smoke, she knows that—but she still won't advance. *I can't, I want to, but I can't*, that's the burden of her speaking look. Meanwhile music in fits and starts, meanwhile stasis as the hissed commentary of departing guests sinks into silence, meanwhile the growing accusation in the eyes that meet her own: *You know I know you know it's just an excuse...*

War Bride (America the Beautiful)

She comes down the *I'll* all white like the blanked out past she as if to (re)move a groomed groom were the tissue – a little stiff at thirst. Starts turning. On our dime. Stops. Smarts up again breaking hearts in two half turns like the messed-up message machine's missing spindle still sort of. Wordlessly twirled. To a too-too tune made mainly of castles in Spain she marches in March or comes down anyhow dumb in a stunned spin her smart womb lurching... Halts there all salt inventing another gilt-edged excuse to stay here slaying them. *I can see myself there.* Playing. Wired to vanished spires and finished liars, this sway of belle-like skirt skirting the cost of the conflict mutes tongues in a swishy mist of chiffon and tulle, makes a cake walk part of the blast wall after all the what we called meanwhiles. Appeals? O I do as you do approve moved anew by her bearing whose smooth up do does what to a lived to do list darkly crossed through? Like it's her. Whirled. To a refrain made insanely of planes her reign falls mainly on a referred stain. Swirled. *I told you I tried to tell you.* While the winds of this aisle whine through the bars of our unrepresented detainees, plainly in pain she'll tell you they're feigning: kept pets who slept well last when? Waiting. *She's a beaut ain't she boys* buoys her up tight as... End? Bend down now to see how we don't see how and – hey presto – grasp the as yet deferred arrival of that last guest who's always got a good reason why these...too. She comes down right alight like the bill set down on the edge of the table. Collateral. Whoosh, *whose?*

Bride of the Photograph 1940-1944
(ANGLE OF INCIDENCE)

Still in her costume but not fully in her role, as if backstage, appar-
ently unaware she's being snapped: bouquet in one hand and in
the other a cigarette – for instance. Increasingly the bride, like the
soldier, is reified by representations that seem to allow the mask
to slip. Or she is part of the way in which the representations
reify themselves. Suddenly the art is everywhere and nowhere,
impossible to avoid and difficult to locate. As the photographer
invades the formerly private spaces around the event there's a
growing pretence that he or she doesn't exist. As if the images just
presented themselves: leaping into the aperture to emerge in the
developing fluid as if having practiced forever for this moment,
having only waited to be asked.* The rarity is the set joke: bride and
groom biting into the same cookie (he shows his teeth in a grin,
gazing at her across the sugared surface, she glances wide-eyed
back to the camera, lips closed on the crisp edge of the sweet). The
usual mode is the bride captured in the wild, as it were: pensive
in the mirror below the rapt face of the maid who attaches her
headdress, for instance. Where earlier pictures insisted first on
seriousness and then a set happiness, now a spectrum of emotions
is invoked. Lack of awareness of the camera, in this myth, means
the bride's more aware of the complicated feelings attendant on
this change of circumstance. In various settings and poses she
plays them out: sweet melancholy of the farewell to girlhood, etc.,
the shock and awe when she sees herself in the dress, and so forth.
It's as if the candids make the bride real, or more so than the
formal portraits, which were about as useful – as evidence – as the
Hunt of the Unicorn tapestries would be, to prove the existence

---

* Is there a way to talk about photographs without slipping into that out-
dated poetry voice we were already tired of or rather tired with when it first
appeared? The sound of fatigue was part of the seduction. We still use words
like "gentle" and "infinitely," we still go on and on about the light. We like to
say "we," we like to say, "the war," as if there were just one, infinitely gentle
in a burnished distance....

43

of that beast. Here she is: one white-gloved hand outstretched for her falling veil, her face completely obscured by the uniformed groom who bends her backward in what is always already a goodbye embrace. The cloudlike dress was contested territory: if silk for a formal wedding "raised the moral of the troops," as the industry claimed, it was also needed to drop them (softly) behind enemy lines – each wedding gown is a potential parachute. So this slithery whisper as her undone dress slides to the floor conjures other night raids. So both the 'chute and the dress are bundled up and (like the soldier and bride) disappear after their use. Wadded back into the deployment bag, or stiff in its long box, cleaned and preserved in the "heirloom process." Our daughter will wear it. Our son will wear it. Out.

Bride of the Waters

Nods yes, standing in the shallow pool, rocks back on her heels, spouts a clear stream of *I do*s at the ceiling and then falls forward, her head a bubbling hollow: a fountain, mechanical – the sound track now the ugly glug glug glug of her secluded refilling. "What have you got for me" is the question she collapses on, drooling, her face, from the pressure of so many kisses, almost flat, "I have nothing do you hear me nothing for myself" is the phrase that sends her reeling back. "But it's you I love" starts the forward tilt again and her affection spewing forth. I do I do I do I do.... Water hitting water beats a brief foam of lace around her feet. Clunk. "Nothing, nothing," the almost inaudible (under the gay splashing of others in the pool) squeak of the mechanism itself. Then "I glug glug glug you" and she's off again or on – open your umbrellas! Prepare to be doused for a glimpse of her gaze, tender but fixed, and her mouth, rusted into a smooch. Where are your rubbers? It's so easy to mistake these oscillations for progress in the churning water, and then, disappointed, to say she is, we all are, "borne back against the current" this hissing jet of ejected love makes, slapping down all around us. Oh these outpourings we say, righting the craft, so generous, so (clunk) cherished: lucky we had on these life jackets! We steer our frail bark between these massive nodding visages, "now sheering off from this monster directly across our route..., now edging away from that...." At first all we want is to be thoroughly wetted down by her oops, but pretty soon we just hope to escape being drowned in it. "I have nothing," she wails in the distance (if we've made – for the moment – our escape), "nothing!"; faintly we hear her recorded voice following us, "yes I said yes."

Instant Bride

A scatter of tipsy laughter floats off from the open convertible floored toward the drive-thru chapel. Take a notion to be together forever? Got a sudden itch to decide the rest of your romantic life? If this is true love why wait another minute to make it official? The courthouse is open 24/7, there's this strip of charming venues and any number of sweating Elvis impersonators to waddle up (*late* Elvis) and officiate. When you can't wait 48 hours much less three whole days to be hitched, a greasy wisp of plastic lace suggests veil, gown, and hymen; one long-stemmed red rose nods toward everything a crowded bouquet loudly asserts. If stolen kisses are sweeter, better than any long-prepared catered affair must be this small snatched happiness. The whirl of *Will you, right now?* The tumble of *Why not?* collapsing into *Yes!* Then the giddy introduction to a couple of "guests" whose names we can immediately forget: strangers always make the best witnesses! To hell with the blood test, baby, let's cut right to I do and be done with it! What larks! Set loose into thinnest instant fantasy life in Elkton, Yuma, Gatlinburg or Las Vegas. Should it be the Little Church of the West? Or the Chapel of the Flowers? Kiss the bride! Hurry! Let's get this over with! Let's file a joint return, let's change our legal status! Why wait? A bump precedes the girl entering in a borrowed gown let out: might there be "a little blessing" to legitimate? We eloped, we'll say, your mom and dad eloped – O it was so *Romantic!* O the rush as idea becomes action and nagging doubts are left in the dust! O to move at last at what seems like pleasure's speed, that cinematic velocity we always believed our lives would accelerate into someday: free of waiting rooms and traffic jams, spangled with bright anticipations that wink and – as our wishes are immediately granted – go out (only to be replaced by the glitter of even more thrilling desires)! O to dash at joy, which appears to disappear so fast! If the formal wedding's a sort of novel then this (taking the plunge! jumping the broom! tying the knot!) is a sonnet, or maybe more like an excerpt from an Opera put on by a small ensemble, in the middle of nowhere, from the back of a truck? All suggestion: not just pared down but compressed to its essence – to love honor comfort and okay get on with it will ya? *What's taking so long?* Chuck the rice that came with this package so we can get back to the honeymoon suite! Step on it! Tomorrow and tomorrow and tomorrow close the distance, slow but inexorable, heavy and slow and dull and completely unstoppable: the crying jag on the drive to Mexico or Reno, the ugly custody battle, the doctor coming back to sit down beside you, opening the file, saying, "We need to talk about these results."

White Bride Made of Breath

Bride of the Bayou

She is drained – that's her word. She takes care of other people's needs all day long, never thinking of herself, but employing the various time-saving devices developed to expand each task until it approaches the horizon of the impossible. An entire ecology damaged, possibly irreparable: where there were birds no bird, and so forth, the grim countdown of what should be visible. Sticky mud and silence, the tour boat tilted up against the bank below the reopened bar because there's no longer a reason to teach anyone anything about this disappearing world. She seemed, once, so wild *and* tame, so exactly the right combination of unspoiled and viewable, adventurous and predictable. Now no one leans over a guardrail to watch the reflected sky ripple past, alert for the first glance of a lazing reptile in her shadowed shallows – all that water flowed away through the gates opened to make her (to development) accessible. Now anyone with money can find their own purpose for...if they want to: space made by the erasure of wetlands and wildlife is designated useful. As if the zone of pity and contempt she soon comes to occupy ("Oh mother, *really*!!") helps those around her live safely outside of that zone? For how long? But this was a bride once! And now weeds rise in the empty parking lot among fading "For Sale" signs. "Brides are the focus of such outpourings of love and joy," one who should know remarks, "but nobody cares for the newlywed." First it's the high cost of cleaning the dress and then the problem of finding offspring to admire and resurrect the age-stiffened silhouette. Use your imagination – recreate among dying trees stuck in cracked silt the shapes of dead and gone things: etch claws and fins and scales into earth, cut the sky into wings – agitate stillness. Then fasten a slow unreadable gaze to a rough grayish green slick afloat in the murk, as the bride turns, almost at once, into the wistful, increasingly edgy, wife...on her way to becoming the more or less gently resentful mother, scrubbing down the toilet with a wad of filthy lace.

Born Again Bride

A fluff of mythic down emerges from the ashes of a former self
consumed by regrets and apologies. White as any fresh start the
BAB sashays one step at a time up an aisle that seems always to
keep getting longer and yet less difficult. But I won't she says. I
was I mean I am which means I did but now I don't. You need
to forgive me now it's that step. On her delicate but stiff neck
her aching head swivels so she doesn't have to move the blood-
shot eyes she's keeping almost shut against what seems like
the unendurable brightness of her own dress. Meanwhile the
wreckage behind her flares and smokes. She's rimmed in light
as if airbrushed on midnight blue velvet and the wedding march
almost covers the screams and weeping in the burnished distance
or those sounds are gathered up to become part of the melody's
endless crescendos dahdahdahdahhhhh etc. That wasn't who I
really was but this is really she says invoking various prepositions
to locate truth behind or underneath I was this pure she winks this
trusting this always this. Innocent. I've changed. You have just
got to believe that. I'd do it differently now, of course, you know I
would and now if you could just.... The tears of those who weep to
see her saying this puddle and flood the venue as if the problem
were, as she once claimed, our too ready sympathy, our haste to
say – *with* her – Hey nobody's perfect, our never mind dear ever-
ready willingness to just go along with the next.... Hoping for the
best. It's probably for the best. The oily water rises to our chins
and keeps pouring in while she... – she floats off, her bubbling
skirts puffed out by promises she swears she'll keep this time (of
course, sure, like duh, you can count on it, just stop shouting at
me) to surge past the death do us part part

White Bride

Blank page. It's this dress – I can't breathe in it. Deep flounces of colorless fabric mount as if trying to reset a clock, a wake, our task to look back and not look back. Salt at the wrist – then up the arm to the shoulder, all the way to the bitter white heart. Bandaged: existing as erasure, I appear where I disappear. It's a costume or an heirloom or it's both. It's a copy: it's unique. It will only be worn once, and then it was only worn once: on the most important day of.... Then it's listed among unclaimed gowns at the cleaners or crushed into a corner of the thrift shop. "I pretended I was in a play," she confesses, speaking of her wedding, "I'd done theater – I knew how to get through it." Colorless scentless sift of time and this feeling of connection to events we didn't experience then this sense of being disconnected from what in fact... And elected – representative. "I wish I'd put it on before and learned how to walk around in it." Unmarked or almost: maybe a smudge of dust or a faint smear of what looks like rust at the edge of – but you'd have to know where to look. Because it cost too much to clean it. "Regrets? I wish I'd known how hard my dress would be to move in...I would've practiced."

Bride Tide

As among the many possible mistakes (from choosing a hideous dress to marrying exactly the wrong person), the fall is always first – begin there, O muse: with the unintentional. Try the slip, the spill, the drop, and the sprawl: the reversal of north and south, the up-ending of the world, the big oops. Start by melting to the floor as if fainting and ask members of the party to also sway, tilt, and slowly crumple as if blasted by an invisible raygun in some long ago low budget science fiction flick. The thud of bodies hitting the ground should drown out the Mendelssohn, until the organist also slumps over, grinding one last chord to an off-key wheeze. Then jazz it up: try the trip, the splits, the tumble, and the pratfall, give roller skates a go! Grease the stairs or scatter little unwrapped guest soaps in your special colors throughout the venue (carry bouquets of swirled "roses" of sterile gauze, each gemmed by dewdrops of antibiotic ointment). Have children from former marriages toss banana peels into the aisle. Ice the walkways! All you need is cold weather and a hose, this look is a knock-out! Try having the bride wear cleats and letting everyone else just slip around: this is a stunning effect, chic and casual; penguins make excellent ring-bearers and a little jacket of polar bear fur for the BT is the perfect touch. To carry out your theme, be sure to use fragile materials: at the end of the ceremony nothing should be left intact! Smeared lipstick is a nice effect, and you'll want broken, not just chipped, nails. Ideally the groom's stutter should resurface, and the bride should be so heart-stoppingly long in her response to the crucial question that that the sound of her mother passing gas is clearly audible. If you can find a friend or family member willing to stand up and fuss at the proper moment, great, but (because this is a super place to make a statement) it's completely worth it to hire a professional: you can tell him or her exactly how long the objection should be and how detailed, you can ask for the something special, maybe scatological. Trust your vendors! Let a backsliding priest or lapsed rabbi make foolish hash of your names, let him (or her), look bored and impatient: in the yellow, blurry pictures you should still be able to see a contemptuous smirk. Do find the most distracted, sulky, and already (how did she do it?) filthy flower girl: little fairy of the will-resisting real – let her stomp in first, flinging loose beads, beans, ball bearings or marbles. Film, O muse, the fatal misstep that lands the bride in the pool, and the groom plunging in to join her, not rescue. Let them be married like that: shaken but, for just this moment, fear-less... – soaked through.

Crossways Bride of the Enthusiastic Do-It-Yourself

We go a lowercase disturbed around here when we become cross-ways a enthusiastic DIY send and this digit has us chomping at the taste to deal every of the sexy details. Eden locate unitedly a patterned how-to for TWO assorted ornament ideas that are not exclusive uber artful and smart but also unbelievably cushy budget friendly. The prizewinning conception is you crapper ingest meet digit of these ideas for a chic recent countenance or intermixture them up for more of an philosopher vibe. You rattling can't go criminal with these babies.

#1 Supplies: older cans / nonfunctional essay / adhesive

1) Start aggregation cans, every assorted sizes, verify your friends and kinsfolk to spend them for you.

2) Find some beautiful, exalting essay that fits your circumstance motif. This is where you crapper rattling appearance the counte-nance and see of your ornament meet by effort fictive with the paper. If you're rattling opinion brave you could modify ingest cute smart fabric.

3) Cover the crapper with the paper manoeuvre and revilement the lowermost to sound the crapper perfectly.

4) Attach the essay to the crapper acquire using a blistering glue cement or tape! If the essay doesn't sound every the artifact around ingest digit sheets or intend fictive and ingest buttons alter or some added you poverty to counterbalance the gap!

5) Fill the crapper with simple foppish flowers and permit the vase do the talking!

I utilized cardinal albescent roses to modify this vase. They were every revilement at an seek and settled in the can. So simple but rattling magical and cushy to do!

#2 Supplies: wooden incase / impressible activity / patterned foam

1) Purchase a wooden box. We institute ours at Ikea for a whopping $5.99.

2) Start aggregation impressible bags from stores. Each incase module ingest digit impressible bag. Make trusty there are no holes in the impressible bag. Then, locate the lowermost exclusive the incase and revilement downbound the sides.

3) Cut a example of patterned sparkle so it module sound nicely in the in the box. Before you locate the sparkle exclusive the box you'll requirement to consign it in liquid until it becomes onerous and filled. Then locate it exclusive the activity and into the box.

4) Be fictive and ingest some flowers your hunch desires. In this centerpiece naif and albescent Asiatic Spider Mums were used as substantially as naif filler. Once you hit your flowers meet move playing! Floral sparkle is so recreation because it allows you to care your flowers meet the artifact you want. Press the stems of the flowers into to the sparkle and the flowers module take from the liquid the sparkle soaked up. By using patterned sparkle you module hit more curb where you locate apiece individualist flower.

Phantom Bride of the Iron Ways 11

DECK 'EM!

We're not saying you should spend a gazillion dollars on 20-foot high barbed wire-topped blast walls, but first impressions are important, so take time to think out the entrance to your green zone. Add a couple IED arrangements to the route or ask embedded photojournalists to create a stylish display of graphic images. Kiosks at the checkpoints with engagement photos, your parents' war albums, and other artifacts make meaningful additions.

LIGHTEN UP!

Revolutionize the territory with creative lighting. Project falling bombs or helicopters to add drama to a boring, beige war; add a funky stylized map or a scrolling list of names in white phosphorus; use tracers or get basic up-lighting for the perimeter to instantly transform the space. Go for a retro look with a Shake and Bake. Your enemies won't be able to stop staring (in a good way!).

STOP THE SHOW!

If you play it right, your exit will be one of the most heavily photographed moments of your war – so forget the leaflets and MREs. Jazz up your exit by passing out small bags of colorful anthrax and ricin, paper airplanes, sugar warships, or even hand grenades for everyone to toss your way. Even better: Stage your own mini parade by passing out hellfire missles and asking guests to escort you to your getaway car or armored vehicle.

FACE THE MUSIC!

Sure, the whistle of incoming ordnance is nice, but you'll blow guests away with a trio of homemade explosives or a well-stocked suicide bomber. To get a conflict going in an off year, look into hiring mercenaries, psychopaths, or a quartet from Blackwater for some seriously memorable sounds.

A Dress Change!

All eyes will be on you, so it'll be a huge shocker when you go from classic ACU for the conflict to flirtier camouflage for the occupation. Whether it's a Chemical Protective Undergarment you bought (but couldn't find an excuse to wear) or a sparkly, white paramilitary outfit that's just too short for the war on terror, have fun with it! If you honestly can't imagine changing out of your uniform, make other changes: let down your hair, switch boots for sandals, or loot a few new pieces of jewelry.

In the Drink!

Grab adversaries' attention as soon as they arrive by having tortured bodies displayed on ice or placed along the shelves of a makeshift bookcase-turned-morgue. Have a private security detail standing at the entrance, ready to greet dissidents at the door. When the mood is right, serve your signature Molotov cocktail in monogrammed bottles. The message will be clear: It's time to par-tay.

Sign On!

If it's an outdoor conflict, create rustic wooden signs in your colors as pointers for allies and enemies ("come to the insurgency" or "war this way!"). For a more formal conflict, make beautifully scripted toe tag numbers, hand-decorated body bags, and even door labels for siege situations labeled "us" and "them."

Picture This!

Having a photo booth is a surefire way to capture memories even embedded photographers might miss. For an extra-special touch, outfit your booth with themed props to get your allies in the mood (snorkel gear and an under-the-sea backdrop for island warfare, opera gloves and M80s for a formal affair set in Europe, leashes and a mutilated Koran for a middle eastern-themed event, etc.); be sure to include copies of pictures after the retreat, when you do a final air drop of thank-you notes.

Do Us a Favor!

Think of souvenirs as accessories to your occupation. Want a packed insurgency? Disband the militia and give them access to unlimited weapons for a good time that just won't quit. Use war trophies as a way to punch up the discomfort level: share compromising snapshots of detained combatants with guests who love to shut down the checkpoints; distribute cozy hoods to fend off the chill of evening torture.

Let 'em Eat Improvised Explosive Devices!

Find the right bomb maker and go nuts with your IEDs and booby traps for a unique photo op: we've seen everything from elaborate rubble to food stalls to camels, carcasses, and even children. Hand out trigger devices – monogrammed cell phones are super – so your guests control the fun right up to the moment of initiation. Other ideas: set out warm doughnuts over a cache of UXOs, or consider hiring an ice cream truck bomb.

Dance It Off!

Take a few lessons, but instead of the standard war, kick it up a notch by learning a sultry occupation or high-energy swing invasion. For an unexpected surprise, get your dad or even your grandpa in on the act. Imagine the looks on your enemies' faces when you and your pops break into a hip-hop routine in the middle of hostage negotiations. (Bonus points if he can do the worm!)

Get Your Best Reception!

Give enemies a place to mingle between operations by creating a lounge area or detention center. Fence off discrete areas, but keep sightlines open. It's the perfect way to keep everyone in on the party even when they're resting. Really want to wow 'em? Make a separate space for interrogations or close off an area with curtains to create a VIP vibe.

SNACK ATTACK!

Just when everyone thinks the fun is winding down and the war might even be over, liven up the party with late-night nibbles that will leave everyone ready for an extended conflict. Think about it: bribes and favoritism, dubious reconstruction contracts, varieties of political corruption, a disordered and ineffective legal system, failing infrastructure...and a permanent base loaded with chocolate chip cookies and milk shooters!

FROM HERE TO ETERNITY!

Come up with a transportation plan that'll get enemies talking. Maybe your war-obsessed uncle would be willing to play driver in exchange for showing off his ridiculously cool Hornet. Your oversized Chinook from Vietnam might actually look pretty cool decked out with streamers and a "just warring" sign. Even a late model Humvee – Frankensteined, uparmored – could create a memorable exit.

A WEBSITE FOR SORE EYES!

Start the party long before your war begins with a brilliant conflict website (computer science degree not required). Upload vlogs (aka video blogs) of your diplomatic failures, poll allies on the reception music, add animated elements, or even create an "enemy of the week" spotlight column. Start your page on (ahem) GWOT. com or get the souped-up version on ConflictTracker.com ($50, but *soooo* worth it!)

Bride of the New Dawn

She appears to be recognized as herself and not herself, new because endlessly recycled, not what she was but not what she will be – see? Not married and not not married, the processional's a ritual meant to extend a magical present, until the head of this pin is the size of a rented hall and all of us angels stepping out on the long blank train of her on-going gown. To go in single and come married out is easy enough, what matters is to enlarge the interstitial, to live as long as we can in the not exactly no longer and the not quite not yet also. Where organ music drowns the ill-digested vows and the empty stomach growls. Hesitant. The BND goes down slow as a pill we can't really swallow, stuck chunk in a stalled gulp between yesterday and tomorrow, at one and the same time belated and punctual. It's the system itself we've come to see (open the plug of that rubber-edged rose window), not me and not you, but we: the marriage of church and state made visible, audible, available. Here *Dearly Beloved's* an embarrassing gurgle, and the costly gown so much densely crumpled bathroom tissue backing up one overworked way in and out of the usual world. From the mouth to points South, scrawl that in soap on the vehicle? From "will you?" to "why don't you ever?" on the march to "irreconcilable." Hey – whoa! Away with you hand-wringing nay sayers: be here now now now now.... Cheeks are flushed and eyes overflow as we grasp her new handle, here to hear the I do as a couple of hard blows: that flesh-blunted sound of bone on bone dislodging as cough a caught morsel not thoroughly chewed. Back out, back up, quagmire, circle: proposed solutions involve the usual budget expansions, extended tours of duty, and additional troops.

Machete Harvest, Mandarin Squeeze, Marne, Marne Avalanche, Marne Grand Slam, Marne Piledriver, Marne Rugged, Marne Torch, Market Sweep, Matador, Moon River Dragon, Mutual Security, Mustang Flex, Mustang Socko. National Unity, New Dawn, New Market, Northern Delay, Northern Fury, Northern Lights, O.K. Corral, Olympus, Open Window, Option North, Outer Banks, Outlaw Destroyer, Overcoat, Panther Backroads, Panther Squeeze, Passage, Pegasus Bridge, Peninsula Strike, Phantom Fury, Phantom Linebacker, Phantom Phoenix, Phantom Strike, Phantom Thunder, Planet x, Plymouth Rock, Polar Black Diamond, Polar Charade, Polar Dive and Polar Dive II, Polar Scrum, Polar Tempest, Powder River, Predator, Punisher III, Purple Haze, Quickstrike, Quicksweep, Raging Bull and Raging Bull II, Ramadan Roundup, Rapier Thrust, Rat Trap, Red Bull and Red Bull II, Red Dawn, Relentless Hunt, Resolute Sword, Restore Peace VI, Restoring Rights, Rifles Blitz, Rifles Fury, Rifle Sweep, Ripper Sweep, Rising Force, River Blitz, River Falcon, River Gate, River Walk, Roaring Tiger, Rock Bottom, Rock Drill, Rocketman, Rocketman III, Rock Hammer, Rock Reaper, Rock Slide, Rogue Stomp, Rogue Thunder, Saber, Saber Guardian, Safety and Security, Sand Storm, San Juan, Santa, Scorpion, Scorpion Sting, Scrimmage, Seahorse, Shadyville, Showdown, Sidewinder, Silverado, Sledgehammer, Slim Shady, Soda Mountain, Soprano Squeeze Play, SOUK, Spring Break, Steel Curtain, Sunset, Spartan Scorpion, Spider Web, Spring Cleanup, Strategic Separation, Stampede 3, Striker Hurricane, Striker Tornado, Suicide Kings, Swarmer, Swashbuckle, Sweeny, Tangerine Pinch, Tangerine Squeeze, Telic, Thunderstruck, Tiger Care, Tiger Clean Sweep, Tiger Fury, Tiger Hammer, Tigers, Tobruk, Together Forward, Tombstone Piledriver, Trailblazer, Trifecta, Triple Play, True Grit, Turki Bowl and Turki Bowl II, Tuwaitha Sunrise, Tyr, Unforgiven, Unified Fist, Unified Front, Vacant City, Vanguard Thunder, Vigilant Resolve, Viking Snatch, Vipers Bite, Warhorse Whirlwind,

Warrior, Warrior Resolve, Warriors Rage, White House, White Rockets, White Shield, William Wallace, Wolfhound Fury 11, Wolfhound Power, Wolfpack Crunch, Wolf Stalk 11, Wolverine, Wolverine Feast, Wonderland, Woodshed, Woodstock...

Dithery Bride of the Word Choice

Abandon or *jilt?* Leave her to her own devices! We request no the pleasure of your company is requested to share our joy no to celebrate.... Discard relinquish swear off – frenzied and zealous. Request the honor of your presence and the favor of a reply if you will worship with or witness. Kindly. We'll have to pull the trigger on the color of the ink in the next few weeks. Numbers spelled out. Honored to have you share in the joy of. She hesitates. The DBWC or RB is born and raised and lives excited to precarious stasis in those instants that teeter on the edge of irrevocable decision. Yes no no yes. Electrified by the bright buzzing shimmer of her selection's importance. "If," she says, and again, "if." And then "or." Then "this no this." Her free will flutters wildly tearing its wings on the bars of the cage of recorded etiquette. What I wanted drifts of fluff. And be our guest and afterward at the reception. In thought. Leave undone and also excess. Fate? Often issued in the form of a personal note. Flowers and birds bows and spangles flounces and ornate beadwork appear in the air around her and vanish white on white on white and her long silk train yet pours from the limo as she nears the altar still uncertain who it was exactly she finally settled on to face. The pleasure of. Carelessness. That. Which. Back and forth because it matters is material. "There are circumstances when the bride very much wants to include the name of the deceased parent. This is acceptable, as long as the invitation does not appear to have been issued by the deceased." Quit disregard cease dismiss. At half past surrender please RSVP.

Bride of the Photograph 2009

The invitation. Bride having her hair and makeup done. The gown and the shoes. Bride's bouquet. Bridesmaids or mom buttoning up / zipping the gown. Bride getting ready in the mirror. Bridesmaids reacting to bride in her gown. Groom getting ready / somebody pinning on his boutonniere or tying his tie. Bridal party and family members walking down the aisle. Groom waiting for the bride to come down the aisle. Bride and her escort coming down the aisle. Groom's face when he sees bride. Father giving away his daughter. Bride and groom at altar or chuppah. Exchanging vows. Parents and guests watching the ceremony. Special moments during the ceremony (e.g., candle lighting, breaking the glass). The kiss! Bride and groom coming back up aisle. Couple leaving the ceremony and being showered with rice, flower petals, bubbles, etc.. Portraits (couple alone, with wedding party, with parents, and with family). Multigenerational shots (e.g., bride, mom, and grandma). Guests mingling during the cocktail hour. Bride and groom arriving at reception. Bride and groom greeting guests. Reception tables before guests arrive. The band. First dance. Bride dancing with her father. Groom dancing with his mother. Wide shot of guests on dance floor. Kids having fun. Grandparents and other older guests. Friends and family making toasts. The couple reacting to toasts. The cake. Cake cutting. Bouquet toss. Bride and groom leaving reception. The couple having a private moment.

Bride2B (Brief)

Like a busted lawyer who, knowing the case is lost, must represent herself: do I have to admit I'm conflicted? There's a motion... forward...and then everything – quivering – halts. As if, if I ever existed, my crime was something like avoidance: not apprehended, I can't be released? And yet I confessed? I said I thought you loved the way I kept checking the mirror to see how the moves worked, though now (snow blind in the glare of endless interrogations) I have to almost shut my eyes in order to look: in order to look more *like*. I sign. I strip: I make the expected face (mouth open, eyes closed), quoting a moan and quickly sliding off these sheets; willing to settle, just not to call it that, scheduling further withdrawals and redeployments, acting out some version of innocence or practicing a "lascivious" wink. I'm bound to appeal – at some point. I call my last witness, and another after that; I take the fifth – for life. There's an impulse, some momentum, then a slight drag leading up to the restraining order: then an effort, again, grinding, to get beyond that – everything oscillates a rusty instant before pitching toward the next arrest. I haven't had access to my client but I can assure you she only wanted what she thought you wanted: it wasn't her idea to out-source the actual sex. Our closing arguments are not transparent but translucent: glimpses of further layers of evasion and a distant suggestion of flesh, *Mmmmmmhmmmm*. O, yes. Or so we thought someone thought someone thought it would be good (and good-bye) to attest? We plead not guilty and not not guilty: just a cog in the... *Dis-Missed!* Your honor? I abject.

Colonized Bride (Jewel in the Crown)

("I NEVER GUESSED YOU'D BE SO...POSSESSIVE. NOT AFTER
YOU HAD WHAT YOU WANTED FROM ME, ANYWAY.")

His mouth came down on hers once more, forceful, possessive,
unyielding. This time there was no trace of gentleness in the
lips that ravaged hers

She kissed him, desperate to make him see that he had her, no
matter what. Within seconds, he took over the kiss, grasping
her head to hold her still as his mouth plundered and ravaged
and yes, devoured hers

He muffled her words with a kiss, a long, hungry one that reduced
her to pudding

As his mouth plundered hers with a hunger that answered her own

Then he took her lips with his, his blood fired with the need to
plunder her honeyed mouth

To plunder that lush, supple mouth...[and] plunder that seductive
mouth

The need to brand her with his mouth

He kissed her, plundering first her mouth, then her ear and the
hollow of her throat

Silencing her...he buried his tongue in the sweet hot warmth of her
mouth the way he wanted to bury himself in another part of her

He ravaged her mouth with heady thrusts of his tongue, and when
that no longer satisfied him, he swept his hands down her neck
to shove her gown free of her shoulders so he could strafe her
bared flesh with urgent, openmouthed caresses

He pleasured her with everything he possessed until he thought
he'd burst with the need to bury something other than his
tongue inside her

She seemed perfectly eager to be ravished

Then his mouth seized hers...plundering

If [he] had governed India anywhere as competently as he governed
her body, no wonder everyone lauded his actions

He ravaged her mouth

Dark Matter (PTSD Bride)

(BRIDE OF THE APP)

She doesn't know what to do anymore, she's so lost: she's just sitting here at her computer, crying. She doesn't know what's keeping her from killing herself. *You trained us as killers*...she writes: *no friend, no family, no job...nothing*. She's just so tired of having no one to reach out to – she's not even logging in anymore. The tentacles of the technoworld infiltrate her home. She realizes that the people she used to run with are not really friends – she's back at home and feels more alone than ever. She's looking for a goal she can make for herself, today: maybe she'll take a shower... She's remembering to pray and read her Bible: she's tired of knowledge. If it can go wrong it has. She doesn't know what to believe, she's just not able to trust herself right now: everything she does seems to end in failure...all she wants to do is sleep. Someone said the hospital was an attention-getting "cop-out." All she has left is a deep emptiness inside that constantly eats at every thought. She has a plan to kill herself in a way that she can't be revived or helped – as she commented earlier, it would save taxpayers 30K a year. She's been reported missing. She's going through her breathing exercises. She's listening to friends who say she needs to be safe. She just lost her pet hamster. God knows her struggle. She could be one of the lucky resilient ones who go to hell and back without losing a minute of sleep. In the city the snow isn't pretty after the cars and trucks blacken the snow. Her dad passed away from cancer. Even the place where she had that beautiful uplifting experience with the butterfly has been sold to a private company. What doesn't still her...fakes a danger, wakes an anger, breaks her sonar, sooner, longer, makes a stranger strangler? When she closes her eyes it all happens again. She does appreciate the concern; she's ready to talk about the stigma. The note reads: *This is not accidental...* Still pill chill ill? *Bonkers*. The words here on the slide from Sophocles really tell the story. Her value comes from within.

"The couple having a private moment."

She should be seen being lifted out of sight: on a high trapeze still rising, say, and swinging above the stage, hissing "I hate you I hate you I hate you..." In the dimness far above she whispers spits and mumbles, she shrieks and flings down into the pooled light on the floor the various masks she's been wearing: alternating "beautiful" (carefully made up) faces with monster visages, so lipstick-y smiles flop down along with snarling muzzles or gaping holes fenced with broken brownish fangs dripping reddish froth... "I haaaaaattttteee you!" She trills it out, standing on one foot, still in that silly bird costume they made her wear, singing it. And plop: the blond wig tumbles to the ground and then the brunette wig and so does, shortly, the silver mane and the nest of writhing snakes. *I hate you*, she thinks it hard enough so that it seems to fill the shadowed space, as she hooks her knees over the bar and swings, upside down, back and forth. "I h-aghydpn goooo" we hear (but faintly) as she rips apart the frilled and feathered gown – dropping fake breasts into the sawdust below, thump, floosh – and pulling the luscious rubber ass-mask around and up over her face...

Fugitive Bride

She resists description by not existing where the language
lands – I think you told me that once. Well, sheesh, who does? You
laughed if I remember right insisting this was slightly different
(though, you added that, as usual, words come nowhere near to
it). To say she's a reaction to a reaction is (in media res) a start.
A mechanism. Standing either too far off for even a shred of
wind lifted foam to touch your lips or so close you're constantly
doused and having to – at measured intervals (like clockwork your-
self) – duck, you know you only know a single aspect you wouldn't
"for the world" have anyone else take for the truth. So you say you
said. So you say she gets away, so you require that. Kept on ice
this image of her running off, white skirts gathered in her fists,
pale veil streaked behind her on the sky like a thin drift of cirrus.
She appears in order to vanish: so who here doesn't? Either this
theorizing is all wet or else it's true that you just can't talk about
it – or both? Once upon a time, so the story of the FB begins, you
found yourself alone in a colorless room where light slicked the
plastic-wrapped silhouettes. And someone said Choose, said, It's
your choice. The question was never whether or not to be absent
but only the shape of your absence, the line, the length. Veils
hung white on the white walls so the chamber looked like it
ought to be opened and left for awhile, set on "defrost." In your
heart a flower made of glass, life-like but cracked. On the inside
becoming the outside and vice versa, the mobius dress of the
message, moving toward gold bands whose meaning is both up
for grabs at every instant and never in doubt, here she comes
/ there she goes crying, in either case, for what she swears is
pure happiness. So shut, as the saying goes, your trap. On stage,
in costume, we promise to be true forever: mesh and net, slip
after blank slip. The meaning of each brief manifestation merely
this: each manifestation is brief...and to be repeated. And to be
repeated: we sign the checks and let the children go, we sign
more checks and send the children back again and then sign up

more children, they follow the money and come back changed if they come back. Meantime fatigue at the edge of the long party, little gatherings of the eligible all reaching for the air, anxious for this moment: the chance to snatch a sky blue garter from the sky or grasp a cloud of blooms in tumbling flight.

Bride of the Theater (of Operations)

This contraption – springs, shredded plastic, broken pipe – is The Memory of Hurt: a movable proscenium, most of the action takes place in its confines. The shattered glass on the floor is absolutely necessary to the mood we're trying to set here…you'll just have to learn to be careful.

If you come downstage we'll start with a series of questions while we make sure you are not concealing explosives. Please repeat each question before answering, loudly and clearly: recording devices are hidden in the piles of debris.

How are you ambitious frustrated sorry

This swinging weight's The Addictive Tendency: we lose a few people we feel we can afford to lose, the rest of you ("watch your step") keep track of what you're using.

Movements are stiff and inhibited, gestures at least clumsy and bodies, if not damaged in some way, awkward, probably heavy; if you drew a gold card at the audition you know you'll be allowed at least one Moment of Grace, a silver card means you're Not Unreasonably Hoping, otherwise…

How are you patient how are you forgiving if you are forgiving

The lovers (Romantics), front and center, touch each other as if they had a stiffly illustrated manual in their heads, like mechanics going over unreliable machines: she checks cock balls ass nipples mouth cock (endless repetitions, as if without memory – it's a kind of juggling); he checks tits ass tits ass tits ass mouth tits ass (etc).

Upstage is a wall of cinderblocks interrupted by a loading dock (locked) and one small high barred lightless window. We hear the constant grind of passing traffic.

The lighting is "mood lighting" meaning how are you moody meaning what is your geographical range

The lighting is mostly passing headlights

Anyone who wants to can use the spray paint.

This other frame – white silk flowers and ribbon-wrapped greenery doused in glitter, hung with rose lace and garlands of jeweled keys – is Potential Happiness: it appears upstage briefly at certain moments (shifted by those Not Unreasonably Hoping), at some distance from the action, but mostly the audience is left to guess at or simply have faith in its existence. Sometimes there's a warm glow from just off-stage. Hold it out at arm's length: soaked in toilet water, Potential Happiness reeks.

Watch your step.

How are you pleased if you were ever pleased

At several points in the action we hear the amplified sound of someone swabbing down a staircase, clunk of the bucket, slosh of the water, slap of the mop: coming near and (after seeming right outside a door lightly hit with the edge of the soaking wad of rags or strings) retreating...and then returning – at intervals replaced by the rough whupping of 'copter blades, a recorded crash, and the sound of someone yelling...

Projected above the stage are images of connection (Connection): these clips should include images of the actual lovers, from their "real" lives, but, equally, cut in and out of more or less well-known images from "great art," "pornography," and advertising.

How are you intimate, how were we

Anyone caught using the spray paint will be arraigned.

TVs at the corner of the stage show infomercials for exercise videos that lead to "a perky butt" and close-ups of tweezers pulling shards of glass from bleeding feet, hands and knees. Hydrogen peroxide foaming in the wounds in resembles pinkish lace. Sort of? Don't you think so? I do!

Feminine voiceover (Confession): "Perhaps if I told you that I'd always felt I was hideously ugly, almost a monster, but without that cache, or force, more a collection of flaws, actually, not even a collection but an assembly or haphazard collage or even just a dump of mistakes, a situation I spent my time and energy disguising, trying to decorate, or hopelessly denying..."

The slight figure in the leaf outfit and bird mask, barefoot, never lit directly, patters then limps from actor to actor asking everyone he/she encounters if they're okay (variations include "are you okay," "are we okay," "am I still breathing"...)

As the piece progresses, more and more of the set should be tagged by huge illegible signatures and more or less elaborate versions of dollar signs.

Masculine voiceover (Expression): a recording (played at various volumes and speeds); whenever this voiceover falls silent the words – on-going – appear as "subtitles" flowing over faces and bodies or scrolling in text clumps obscuring portions of the stage. The substance of this Expression is comprised bits of "famous" speeches from Great Men mixed into a tissue of political clichés amid detailed and graphic descriptions of SERE techniques.

The program is blank.

The shadow figures (Shadow Figures) for the lovers ("Love") should be onstage at all times but only lit intermittently. They cannot touch but can use their awareness of the limited perspective of the spectators to appear as "over-lapping." The duet ("Why won't you touch me? I touch you") is constant but performed at wildly various volumes, moving between a whisper (barely more than heavy breathing) and a ragged scream.

The program is not entirely blank: there is a penciled question in one corner

The stage is occasionally almost erased – all action disappearing – by the hard white glare of rising phosphorescent flares.

The program is too blank. Is not. Is so.

Where are you
Where are you frightened or how and where did you

There's a stuck tune playing or starting over and over again in the lobby: You'd be You'd be so You'd be so nice Nice to You'd be To come To come To come

Where did you

I'm not asking how you're angry I know how you're angry

I hold these hands out

Other titles from Otis Books | Seismicity Editions

Erik Anderson, *The Poetics of Trespass*
      Published 2010 | 112 Pages | $12.95
      ISBN-13: 978-0-979-6177-7-5
      ISBN-10: 0-979-6166-7-4

J. Reuben Appelman, *Make Loneliness*
      Published 2008 | 84 pages | $12.95
      ISBN-13: 978-0-9796177-0-6
      ISBN-10: 0-9796177-0-7

Bruce Bégout, *Common Place. The American Motel.*
      Published 2010 | 143 Pages | $12.95
      ISBN-13: 978-0-979-6177-8-2
      ISBN-10: 0-979-6177-8-

Guy Bennett, *Self-Evident Poems*
      Published 2011 | 96 pages | $12.95
      ISBN-13: 978-0-9845289-0-5
      ISBN-10: 0-9845289-0-3

Guy Bennett and Béatrice Mousli, Editors, *Seeing Los Angeles:*
A Different Look at a Different City
      Published 2007 | 202 pages | $12.95
      ISBN-13: 978-0-9755924-9-6
      ISBN-10: 0-9755924-9-1

Robert Crosson, *Signs/ & Signals: The Daybooks of Robert Crosson*
      Published 2008 | 245 Pages | $14.95
      ISBN: 978-0-9796177-3-7

Robert Crosson, *Daybook (1983–86)*
      Published 2011 | 96 Pages | $12.95
      ISBN-13: 978-0-9845289-1-2
      ISBN- 0-9845289-1-1

Mohammed Dib, *Tlemcen or Places of Writing*
      Published 2012 | 120 pages | $12.95
      ISBN-13: 978-0-9845289-7-4
      ISBN-10: 0-9845289-7-0

Ray DiPalma, *The Ancient Use of Stone:*
Journals and Daybooks, 1998–2008
      Published 2009 | 216 pages | $14.95
      ISBN: 978-0-9796177-5-1

Jean-Michel Espitallier, *Espitallier's Theorem*
Translated from the French by Guy Bennett
      Published 2003 | 137 pages | $12.95
      ISBN: 0-9755924-2-4

Leland Hickman, *Tiresias: The Collected Poems of Leland Hickman*
      Published 2009 | 205 Pages | $14.95
      ISBN: 978-0-9822645-1-5

Norman M. Klein, *Freud in Coney Island and Other Tales*
      Published 2006 | 104 pages | $12.95
      ISBN: 0-9755924-6-7

Luxorius, *Opera Omnia or, a Duet for Sitar and Trombone*
      Published 2012 | 216 pages | $12.95
      ISBN-13: 978-0-9845289-6-7
      ISBN-10: 0-9845289-5-4

Ken McCullough, *Left Hand*
      Published 2004 | 191 pages | $12.95
      ISBN: 0-9755924-1-6

Béatrice Mousli, Editor, *Review of Two Worlds:*
French and American Poetry in Translation
      Published 2005 | 148 pages | $12.95
      ISBN: 0-9755924-3-2

Ryan Murphy, *Down with the Ship*
      Published 2006 | 66 pages | $12.95
      ISBN: 0-9755924-5-9

Dennis Phillips, *Navigation: Selected Poems, 1985–2010*
      Published 2011 | 288 pages | $14.95
      ISBN 13: 978-0-9845289-4-3
      ISBN: 0-9845289-4-6

Antonio Porta, *Piercing the Page: Selected Poems 1958 – 1989*
    Published 2011 | 368 pages | $14.95
    ISBN-13: 978-0-9845289-5-0
    ISBN: 0-9845289-5-4

Eric Priestley, *For Keeps*
    Published 2009 | 264 pages | $12.95
    ISBN: 978-0-979-6177-4-4

Ari Samsky, *The Capricious Critic*
    Published 2010 | 240 pages | $12.95
    ISBN-13: 978-0-979-177-6-8
    ISBN: 0-979-6177-6-6

Hélène Sanguinetti, *Hence This Cradle*
Translated from the French by Ann Cefola
    Published 2007 | 160 pages | $12.95
    ISBN: 970-0-9755924-7-2

Janet Sarbanes, *Army of One*
    Published 2008 | 173 pages | $12.95
    ISBN-13: 978-0-9796177-1-3
    ISBN-10: 0-9796177-1-5

Severo Sarduy, *Beach Birds*
Translated from the Spanish by Suzanne Jill Levine and Carol Maier
    Published 2007 | 182 pages | $12.95
    ISBN: 978-9755924-8-9

Adriano Spatola, *The Porthole*
Translated from the Italian by Beppe Cavatorta and Polly Geller
    Published 2011 | 112 pages | $12.95
    ISBN 13: 978-0-9796177-9-9
    ISBN-10: 0-9796177-9-0

Adriano Spatola, *Toward Total Poetry*
Translated from the Italian by Brendan W. Hennessey and Guy Bennett
with an Introduction by Guy Bennett
    Published 2008 | 176 pages | $12.95
    ISBN 13: 978-0-9796177-2-0
    ISBN-10: 0-9796177-3-1

Carol Treadwell, *Spots and Trouble Spots*
Published 2004 | 176 pages | $12.95
ISBN: 0-9755924-0-8

Allyssa Wolf, *Vaudeville*
Published 2006 | 82 pages | $12.95
ISBN: 0-9755924-4-0